THE CHEYENNES

A First Americans Book

Virginia Driving Hawk Sneve

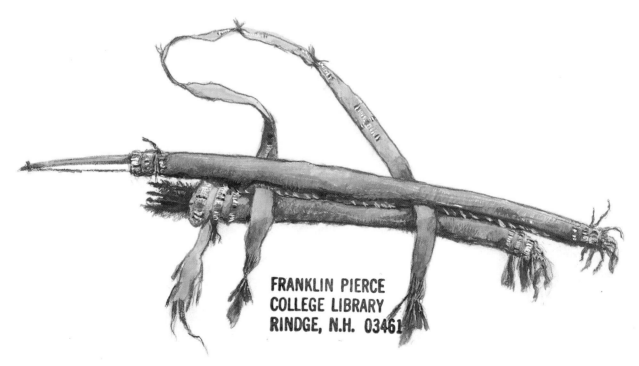

illustrated by Ronald Himler

Holiday House/New York

ACKNOWLEDGMENTS

The Sweet Medicine quotes and the one of the Unknown Cheyenne are from George Bird Grinnell's *The Cheyenne Indians: Their History and Ways of Life,* vol. 2 (New York: Cooper Square Publishers, 1962).

The quote of Porcupine Bear is from T. D. Bonner's *The Life and Adventures of James P. Beckwourth* (New York: Alfred A. Knopf, 1931).

The Little Wolf quote is from Mari Sandoz's *Cheyenne Autumn* (New York: Hastings House, 1953).

The Cheyenne Prayer is from Peter J. Powell's *Sweet Medicine*, vol. 1 (Norman: University of Oklahoma Press, 1969).

The Cheyenne Lullaby is from Natalie Curtis's *The Indians' Book* (New York: Dover Publications, 1968).

The quote of Stands in the Timber is from George Bird Grinnell's *By Cheyenne Campfires* (Lincoln: University of Nebraska Press, Bison Book reprint, 1971).

The Black Kettle quote is from Stan Hoig's *The Cheyenne* (New York: Chelsea House, 1989).

The Little Wolf and Dull Knife quote is from Virginia Armstrong's *I Have Spoken* (Athens: Swallow Press/Ohio University Press, 1971).

The Cheyenne Sun Dance Woman Prayer is printed by permission of Henrietta Mann.

Library of Congress Cataloging-in-Publication Data
Sneve, Virginia Driving Hawk.
The Cheyennes / by Virginia Driving Hawk Sneve; illustrated by
Ronald Himler. — 1st ed.
p. cm. — (A First Americans book)
Includes index.
Summary: Provides an overview of the social life and customs and
history of the Cheyenne Indians.
ISBN 0-8234-1250-4 (hardcover: alk. paper)
1. Cheyenne Indians — Juvenile literature. [1. Cheyenne Indians.
2. Indians of North America.] I. Himler, Ronald, ill. II. Title.
III. Series: Sneve, Virginia Driving Hawk. First Americans book.
E99.C53S63   1996   95-50696   CIP   AC
970.004'973 — dc20

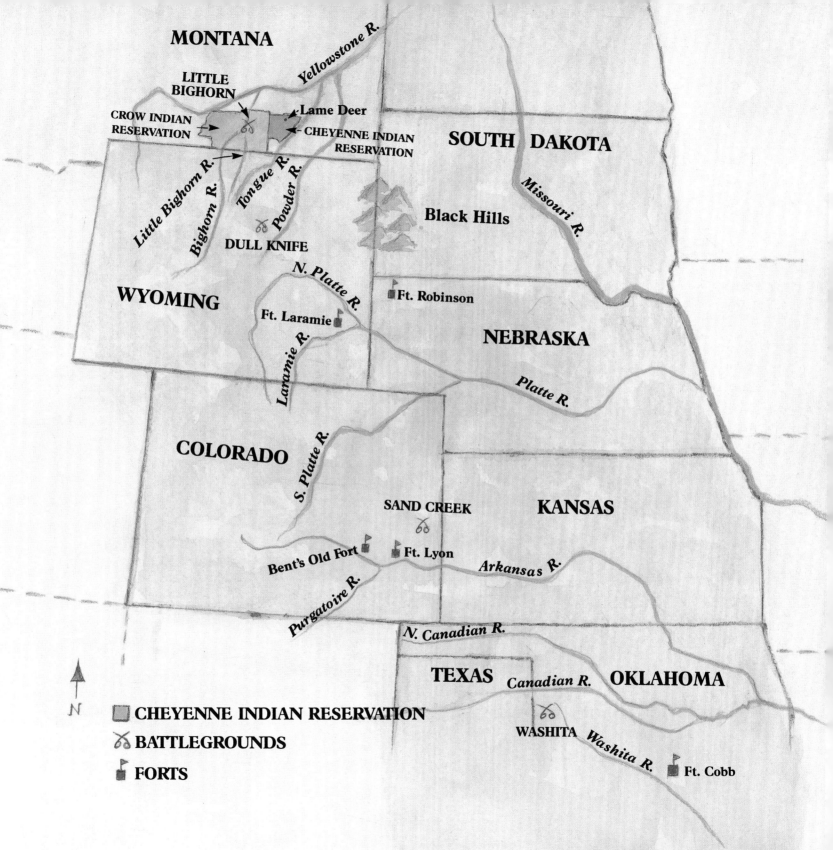

MONTANA

LITTLE
BIGHORN

Lame Deer

CROW INDIAN
RESERVATION

CHEYENNE INDIAN
RESERVATION

SOUTH DAKOTA

Yellowstone R.

Little Bighorn R.

Little Bighorn R.

Bighorn R.

Tongue R.

Powder R.

DULL KNIFE

Missouri R.

Black Hills

WYOMING

N. Platte R.

Ft. Robinson

Ft. Laramie

NEBRASKA

Laramie R.

Platte R.

COLORADO

S. Platte R.

SAND CREEK

KANSAS

Bent's Old Fort

Ft. Lyon

Arkansas R.

Purgatoire R.

N. Canadian R.

TEXAS

Canadian R.

OKLAHOMA

WASHITA

Washita R.

Ft. Cobb

N

CHEYENNE INDIAN RESERVATION

BATTLEGROUNDS

FORTS

CREATION STORIES

*Our Great-grandfather spoke . . . He said he had put people
on this earth, all kinds of people.*

SWEET MEDICINE

The Cheyennes called themselves the *Tse-tsehese-stahase*, "the people." They once lived near the Great Lakes but were gradually forced westward as eastern tribes used guns they got from the white men. Another tribe, the *So'taaeo'o*, had also moved from the lakes area. The two tribes met north of the Missouri River. In the plains the Sioux called the new group *Sha hiye na*, meaning "people of alien speech."

The Cheyennes have two creation stories which reflect their move west. The first may have come from when they lived by lakes.

Long ago water covered all things. The first person floated on the surface of the water. He called to the swans, geese, and other swimming birds, "Bring me some earth from the bottom of the sea."

The larger birds dove, but could not get any dirt. Finally a small duck went down, and after a long while, he swam to the surface with a tiny bit of mud in his bill. The duck put the mud in the person's hand. The person took it and worked it with his fingers until it was dry. Then he placed it in little piles on the surface of the water. Each little pile grew and became land.

After there was firm ground, the person made a man and a woman. Later he created other people to live on the earth.

The second story may have come from the time the Cheyennes lived along the Missouri River.

Once a band of Indians lived in a dark cave. In the distance they saw a light. The people moved toward it and found an opening. They climbed out of the cave into daylight.

They were in a rough country with many rocks and stones. The people did not like the place, so they left. They traveled to a large river with plenty of timber. A star fell from the sky and set fire to the forest. This is how they got fire and learned to use it for cooking and warmth.

MOVING WEST

*Once we were a great and powerful nation: our hearts were proud
and our arms were strong.*

PORCUPINE BEAR

In about 1670 the Tse-tsehese-stahase lived in the Minnesota River Valley.
They were farmers who also fished and hunted. Their enemies, the Ojibwas,
forced the Cheyennes to move west into what are now North and South
Dakota.

In the early 1700s the Tse-tsehese-stahase settled on a river that came to be
called the "Cheyenne."

In 1780 the Ojibwas again forced the Tse-tsehese-stahase to move. The
Mandans and Arikaras helped them cross the Missouri River in bullboats
made of buffalo hides stretched over a willow frame.

Many Tse-tsehese-stahase lived at the Missouri River site in earth houses
built with logs covered with dirt. While they were there, they got horses from
other Indians. The Tse-tsehese-stahase gave up farming and began to follow
the buffalo herds on horseback. They and the So'taaeo'o moved to the Black
Hills area, where they became known as the Cheyennes.

parfleche

bone
spoon

black powder
horn

The Cheyennes adopted the Plains Indians lifestyle. Buffalo meat became their main source of food. They tanned hides into leather for ropes and horse gear. The women stitched several skins together into teepees. They made fur-covered hides into robes, mattresses, and blankets. Moccasin soles and parfleches or storage boxes were fashioned from rawhide. Bones were carved into hide scrapers, knives, and sewing awls. Spoons, cups, ladles, and gunpowder flasks were made from the horns. Bladders served as bags in which quills and sinew were kept. The stomach was a water bag and also a cooking bowl. The Cheyennes stretched it over a wooden frame and filled it with water which was heated with hot stones.

The Cheyennes traveled long distances to trade with other tribes. They took horses, meat, and buffalo robes to the Mandans, Hidatsas, and Arikaras. In return they got corn, dried pumpkin, tobacco, guns, and goods that had come from European traders. They carried these items south and traded them to the Kiowas and Comanches in exchange for horses and brightly striped Spanish blankets.

trading with the Kiowas

The Arapaho and Sioux tribes became friends of the Cheyennes. With these allies, the Cheyennes drove away the Kiowas and Comanches, who had become their enemies when they wanted the buffalo range in western Kansas and Nebraska. By the end of the 1700s, the Cheyennes had traveled west to raid the Crows of the Bighorn River land of Wyoming and Montana; the Shoshones along the Sweetwater River, Wyoming; and the Utes on the eastern slopes of the Colorado Rockies. Their worst enemy, however, were the Pawnees in Nebraska.

MEN

Dog Soldier Society lance

Dog Soldier Society sash

The Cheyenne men were tall and agile. They were brave, hardy warriors, and skilled hunters. They forced themselves to do difficult things so that they would stay in top physical and mental shape.

Every morning the men and boys took a bath in a stream, even in the icy winter waters.

Young men fasted alone for four days on isolated hills. They did this so that they would gain spiritual power. This would allow them to have good fortune and not be hurt in battle.

The men hunted antelope, deer, elk, wild sheep, and buffalo. Using their knees to guide their horses, the hunters would come up close to a buffalo. This freed their hands to hold a bow and arrow to kill the running beast.

Men also trapped wolves and foxes for their fur.

The Cheyennes believed it was a man's duty to go to war. The warriors made frequent raids on enemy tribes to capture horses, or to drive them out of buffalo ranges. When a Cheyenne village was attacked, the warriors defended the women and children or held off the enemy to allow their families to escape.

The Cheyennes had five military societies: Fox, Elk, Shield, Dog, and Bowstring. Each had its own style of dress, dance, and song.

The Dog Soldier Society became famous because it fought many battles against the U.S. Army.

The Cheyenne tribe was made up of ten bands. A band was a group of extended family members. A man could become a chief of his band if he were a skilled warrior and highly respected by friends and enemies. The chief was responsible for peace within his band and with other tribes.

A Cheyenne chief had to be generous, kind, sympathetic, and courageous. He took care of the poor and unfortunate and sometimes even his enemies. He headed a council made up of respected men. The council met to settle disputes and made decisions in the camp.

Four chiefs from each of the ten Cheyenne bands, plus four men who were named principal chiefs, formed a grand council called the Council of Forty-Four. At council meetings, they made decisions affecting the whole tribe.

WOMEN

And bless this young woman and give her a better and longer life as she lives on earth.

CHEYENNE PRAYER

beaded woman's moccasins

woman's dress with cowrie shells

When a young man wanted to marry, he did not ask the girl, but sent an older female relative to her family. The woman took gifts and spoke well of the young man. If the family approved of the suitor, they dressed the girl in her prettiest buckskin dress. Her family put her on a horse, and she was led by an elderly woman to the young man's home. Then the newlyweds moved to a new teepee that the bride's mother had set up near her home.

Some men had more than one wife. But each woman had her own teepee for herself and her children.

Cheyenne women picked berries and dug up wild turnips and other edible roots. They cooked and dried the meat the hunters brought home. They tanned hides and made the teepees. They sewed leather clothing and made moccasins for their whole family. The women trimmed the clothing and moccasins with porcupine quills and, later, beads.

Cheyenne women had no say in council meetings, but they urged the men to do their duty. They also told the men to be careful and not agree to anything that would endanger the tribe.

Sometimes women went to war with the men. Usually they helped with the camp duties. But there were a few women who actually fought alongside the men.

Women had their own societies that were as important as those of the men. The best known was the Quillers' Society. The members made beautifully quilled buffalo robes for honored members of the tribe.

bone scraper

13

CHILDREN

Little good baby, he — ye, Sleepy little baby. A-ha, h'm.
CHEYENNE LULLABY

cradleboard

horse with travois

Babies were carried close to their mothers in cold weather, but placed in a cradleboard when it was warm. The cradle was hung from a lodgepole or placed against the teepee wall. When the women traveled, they hung the cradle from a saddle or travois. A travois was a kind of sled made of lodgepoles fastened behind a horse to carry the teepee, household goods, and sometimes old people and small children.

Children were rarely spanked if they misbehaved. Parents told their children what to do. They warned them against doing something that would be harmful. Children learned that it was important to behave well in order to earn and keep the respect of others.

A child was given a "baby name" soon after its birth. At about age five or six, a child's father arranged for a formal naming ceremony. The father's brother gave a new name to a boy. The father's sister gave a new name to a girl. After the naming, the father presented a horse to the relative who had given the name.

Girls played with deerskin dolls and tiny cradleboards. They cared for the dolls in the same way that their mothers cared for human babies.

Girls learned by watching and helping their mothers and other women in their daily tasks. Older sisters or female cousins also took care of the younger children.

A boy learned to use a small bow and arrows made for him by his father, uncle, or elder brother. He practiced until he never missed a target. Then he and others his age went out to hunt rabbits, turkeys, and grouse.

Girls and boys played together. They set up small teepees and pretended to move camp. They used dogs to pull tiny travois. The boys pretended to protect the girls and their dolls. The boys also had pretend buffalo hunts and horse raids.

Boys and girls learned to ride almost as soon as they began to walk. Older boys herded the band's horses.

When a boy was about twelve, his grandfather instructed him in the duties of being a man. After this a boy would go on his first buffalo hunt. After a successful hunt, a boy could then go to war.

CEREMONY

*Spirits, take pity on me. Send me something for
the people to eat.*
STANDS IN THE TIMBER

eaglebone whistle

buffalo head used in Sun Dance

The Cheyennes gathered in the late summer for the Medicine Lodge Ceremony. The white men called it a Sun Dance. The Cheyennes danced to bring new life to the tribe. When the young men danced, they brought blessings to themselves, their families, the tribe, and the world around them.

The Cheyennes had two important sacred objects. They were the Buffalo Hat and Four Arrows. If they treated the hat and arrows with care and respect, the Cheyennes believed they would have good health, long lives, and plenty to eat. The sacred objects would also give them strength and victory over their enemies.

Sun Dance

The Cheyennes believe Bear Butte, in the Black Hills, is a sacred place. On Bear Butte the Creator gave Sweet Medicine, a Cheyenne holy man, the Four Arrows. He brought them to his people. He predicted the coming of the white men and how the tribe would be moved and changed.

COMING OF THE WHITE MEN

They will try to change you from your way of living to theirs ...
SWEET MEDICINE

Charles Bent

William Bent

Bent's Fort

When the Cheyennes lived in what is now Minnesota, they met the French explorer Sieur de La Salle in 1680. In 1804 the explorers Lewis and Clark found some of the tribe at the Missouri River. They saw others living in the Black Hills of what is now South Dakota.

In about 1825, the Cheyennes split into two groups. The Southern Cheyennes lived along the Arkansas River in southern Colorado. The Northern Cheyennes' homeland was west of the Black Hills in the high country of Wyoming and Montana along the North Platte, Powder, and Tongue rivers. The two groups still maintained family contacts and often moved back and forth between north and south.

In 1828 Charles and William Bent, white fur trappers and traders, met a band of Cheyennes led by Chief Yellow Wolf. The chief agreed to trade with the Bents. The Bents built a fort where the Arkansas and Purgatoire rivers meet in southeastern Colorado. It was known as Fort William or Bent's Fort.

More and more white people were moving through the west. The white men brought whiskey, which made some Cheyennes lose their way because of heavy drinking. The white men also brought diseases which had been unknown to the Indians. In about 1849, cholera killed half of the Cheyennes living in the Arkansas River area. In 1870–72 many Cheyennes died of whooping cough and scarlet fever.

In 1825 the Cheyennes signed the Friendship Treaty with the U.S. government that gave safe passage to whites traveling through Indian land. In return, the government promised to befriend the Indians.

The United States wanted the wars between the tribes to stop because the settlers could not travel when the Indians were fighting among themselves. In 1840 a peace council was held at Bent's Fort. The Cheyennes and Arapahos and their enemies the Comanches, Kiowas, and prairie Apaches met and agreed to be friends.

In September 1851 a treaty council of Cheyennes and nine other tribes — about 10,000 Indians — met at Fort Laramie, Wyoming. The treaty set boundaries for the Cheyennes and Arapahos and other tribes. Under the treaty, the Indians agreed to let the United States build roads and military posts within their territory. In return the government promised to protect the tribes' lands and keep the whites out.

Two years after the treaty of Fort Laramie, 15,000 whites passed through the Indians' land. As a result, there were clashes between the Cheyennes and whites. U.S. Army officers decided that the Indians had to be punished even though the tribes were only defending their land. The whites had broken the promises they'd made in the treaty at Fort Laramie.

The Colorado gold rush of 1859 led to more clashes between the whites and Indians.

SOUTHERN CHEYENNES

All we ask is that we may have peace with the whites.
BLACK KETTLE

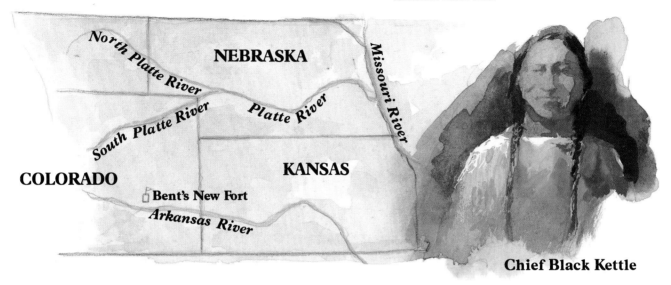

Chief Black Kettle

In 1860, in a new treaty signed at Bent's New Fort in southeastern Colorado, the Southern Cheyennes were assigned to a reservation north of the Arkansas River. In return the government promised them food, clothing, and other goods. The Cheyennes did not like the new reservation. It was too dry for farming, and they couldn't find game to hunt. The Southern Cheyennes were starving. Even though they were angry and depressed at how they were being treated, the Indians tried to remain peaceful. But more and more of the young warriors began attacking wagon trains to get food and supplies for their families.

The U.S. government sent soldiers to stop the raids. The troopers attacked Cheyenne camps in northern Colorado and in western Kansas. At Lean Bear's village, the chief went out to tell the white soldiers that he didn't want to fight. He wore a peace medal and had a note from President Abraham Lincoln that said the chief could be trusted. Lean Bear was shot and killed.

The Cheyennes were angry. The Dog Soldiers struck back by attacking more wagon trains and killing more white men.

Colorado Governor John Evans ordered friendly Indians to come into the U.S. government forts. Chiefs Black Kettle, White Antelope, and Bull Bear believed that if they led their bands into Fort Lyon, they would be safe. In November 1864, the Cheyennes went to the fort. There wasn't enough food for the 652 Indians. Black Kettle's band was told to stay in a camp at the bend of Sand Creek north of the fort.

Colonel John M. Chivington, a commander of the military in Colorado, ordered a volunteer regiment from Denver to march against the Cheyennes. Daylight had just dawned when the troops attacked Black Kettle's camp. The chief raised an American flag and a white flag of peace to show that the camp was friendly, but the troopers paid no attention. Chivington later reported that they had killed from 400 to 500 Cheyennes. Some observers said between 123 to 200 Cheyennes died at Sand Creek. Black Kettle and other survivors escaped and spread word of the massacre to neighboring tribes.

The Dog Soldiers were furious. They led raids against white travelers and settlers. The U.S. government called another treaty council. Now the Cheyennes and Arapahos were told they'd have to move to a new reservation on the Cimarron River in what is now Oklahoma. They had to give up their claim to lands in Colorado. The Dog Soldiers and other warrior groups refused to sign the treaty. The United States sent more soldiers to make them move.

On November 20, 1868, Black Kettle told General William B. Hazen that the Cheyennes wanted peace and would come into Fort Cobb. Hazen said no and sent Black Kettle back to his camp on a stream called the Washita.

At dawn on November 27, 1868, the camp awoke to gunfire and music. Lieutenant Colonel George Armstrong Custer had ordered the Seventh Cavalry's band to play the "Gerry Owen," a stirring march to inspire the seven hundred troopers to fight. Cheyenne women and children were cut down with sabers as they tried to flee. The Cheyenne warriors fought to the death. When the slaughter was ended, more than one hundred Indians were dead and fifty-three women and children had been taken prisoner. Among the dead were Chief Black Kettle and his wife.

The Cheyenne bands scattered. General Philip Sheridan, a military commander in Kansas, ordered forces from New Mexico and Colorado to follow them. The Indians were tired and hungry. Chiefs Little Robe and others agreed to settle on a reservation. The Dog Soldiers, under Tall Bull, resisted until their village and all of their belongings were destroyed, and Tall Bull was killed.

The Cheyennes were starving. Many bands came into the forts and surrendered. The Cheyennes and Arapahos were ordered to a new reservation in central Oklahoma. Small bands of Southern Cheyennes continued to fight, however, until 1875.

NORTHERN CHEYENNES

If you want to fight, I will fight you . . .
LITTLE WOLF AND DULL KNIFE

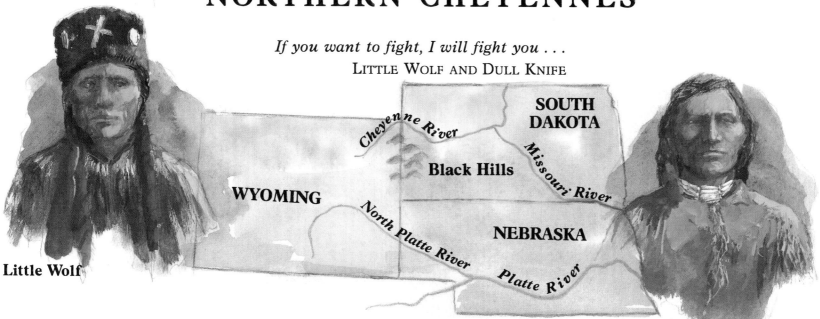

Little Wolf

Dull Knife

In 1859 the Northern Cheyennes, with the Sioux and Northern Arapahos, reluctantly signed a treaty at North Platte Agency, Nebraska. The Indians did not like the way so many white people were moving through their country and killing buffalo and other game. All three tribes had to give up land in western Kansas, Nebraska, and the Dakotas to permit white traffic. The Northern Cheyennes were assigned to a reservation on the Laramie River of southeastern Wyoming.

The Northern Cheyennes resisted the whites passing through the mountains on the way to Utah, California, and Oregon. The U.S. military built forts to protect the whites. But in the 1860s, gold was found in western Montana and hundreds of prospectors came into the area.

In 1866 the U.S. government constructed forts on the Bozeman Trail, which the Northern Cheyennes and Sioux attacked. Little Wolf and Dull Knife were the Cheyenne leaders. Many skirmishes with the troopers occurred until 1868, when the U.S. military moved out of the forts. The Indians burned the forts.

The government set up reservations in Nebraska and Dakota Territory for the Sioux and Northern Cheyennes. But the Cheyennes refused to leave their home in Wyoming.

In 1873 the U.S. government wanted to move all of the Cheyennes to the Southern Cheyenne territory. But the Northern Cheyennes would not go.

In June 1876 thousands of Cheyennes and Sioux were camped on the Little Bighorn in Montana. On the twenty-fifth, Custer, now a general, led an attack on the Indians. His troops were overrun by Sioux and Cheyenne warriors who remembered Custer's raid at Washita. He was killed during the battle.

After the victory, the Cheyennes and Sioux scattered, knowing that they would be pursued by U.S. troops. In November, Dull Knife's camp on the Powder River, Wyoming, was totally destroyed. With no food, horses, or warm clothing, the survivors fled. Many died in a terrible winter. They finally surrendered at Fort Robinson, Nebraska, in April 1877.

The Northern Cheyennes at Fort Robinson were forced to march seventy days to the Southern Cheyenne reservation in Oklahoma. They hated the humid flatlands of the southern reservation. There was little food and much disease. Many Northern Cheyennes died.

Little Wolf and Dull Knife decided to return to Wyoming. On the night of September 7, 1878, 353 Northern Cheyennes secretly crept away. Chased by the military, they battled their way north. Many of them died before they reached the Platte River, Nebraska. The group split. Little Wolf led a small band to the Powder River area in Wyoming and Montana, where they surrendered.

Dull Knife led 150 to the reservation near Fort Robinson, Nebraska. He hoped that his people would be allowed to join their friends, the Sioux, in Red Cloud's reservation. But they were ordered to return to Oklahoma. The Cheyennes refused to leave and were kept prisoner in a large, cold building. They were not given any food or wood for the stoves. The Cheyennes decided to fight and be killed rather than slowly die in the building. Even though only a few warriors had weapons, the Cheyennes made a wild dash for freedom. Sixty-five were recaptured, and fifty froze to death. Some of them were returned to Oklahoma. Others managed to find refuge with the Sioux in Dakota Territory.

TODAY

The great power put the earth here, and must have put us on it. Without the earth nothing could live.

UNKNOWN CHEYENNE

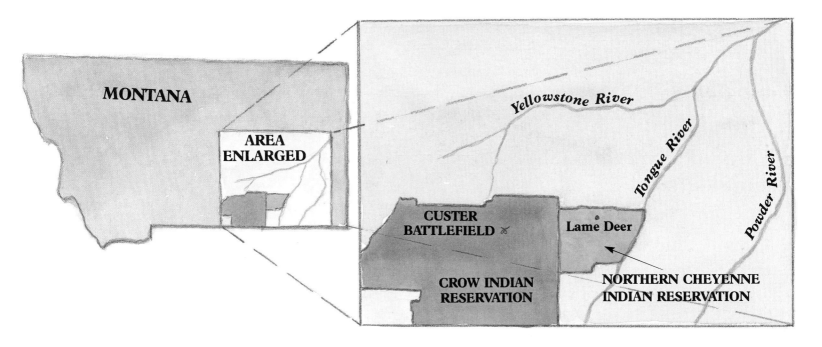

Today the Northern Cheyennes live on a reservation between the Tongue River and Crow reservation in Montana.

In the 1960s coal was found on the Northern Cheyenne reservation. Coal corporations and the Bureau of Indian Affairs signed leases for mineral rights without the Cheyennes' consent. But the coal companies planned to strip-mine the coal. Educated Cheyennes knew that this would destroy the land. With the help of Indian lawyers, much of the Cheyenne rights were returned, and the coal and power companies had to promise to protect the land.

Lame Deer, Montana, is the site of the Northern Cheyennes' tribal agency. Also at Lame Deer is the Dull Knife Memorial College, where high-school graduates and adults continue their education.

29

Many of the Northern Cheyennes are ranchers. Others are employed by the coal companies and the tribal bingo hall. Some Cheyennes are trained as firefighters who are often called to help put out western forest fires. The tribe manages a buffalo herd. There are several celebrations or powwows that take place during the year on the reservation. At the Custer Battlefield National Monument east of Busby, Montana, the Cheyennes hold peace ceremonies.

In Oklahoma, the Southern Cheyennes and Arapahos no longer have a reservation, but share trust lands of some 85,000 acres near the Canadian River, west of Oklahoma City. Nearby, in the Black Kettle National Grassland, is the Washita Battle Ground Historic Site. The tribes' headquarters are in Concho, Oklahoma.

Gas and oil were discovered on Cheyenne and Arapaho land. Some Cheyenne youth are being trained as managers for the tribes' resources.

Both Northern and Southern Cheyennes work as lawyers, teachers, and in other professional occupations as well. They still believe that if they care for the sacred Buffalo Hat and the Four Arrows, the Cheyennes will prosper.

Great Spirit One above
Grandmother Spirit below
We thank you for life and for each new day.
We thank you for our children and for the old ones.
We pray that you bless each Cheyenne with strength, good-heartedness,
    a clear mind, and long life.
We pray that all Cheyennes remember their sacred connection to each other
    and bring blessings of health, beauty, and goodness to themselves and
    all life.

PRAYER OF A CHEYENNE SUN DANCE WOMAN

deerskin shield cover

INDEX